Be a Green Star

Written by Teresa Heapy

Collins

It is clear the planet is getting hotter. Gases form a blanket that traps hot air near to the planet.

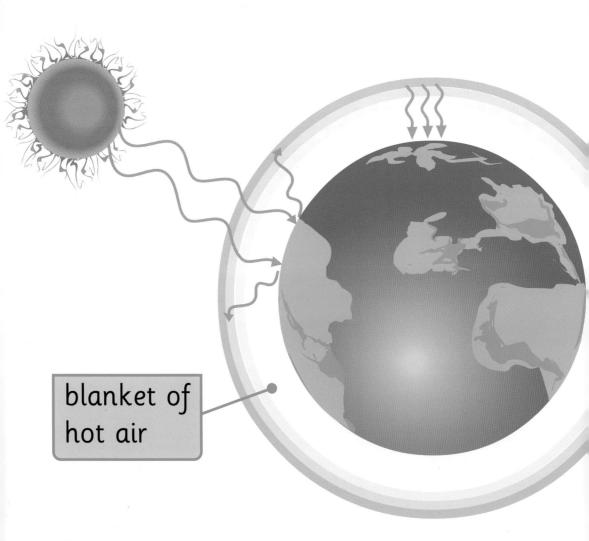

blanket of hot air

This starts lots of problems such as:

rivers bursting banks

melting in the Arctic

getting thinner

shrinking coasts

trees getting burnt

The planet is under strain. The clock is ticking! So how can we help? We can start to think greener and smarter!

We can shift from oil and gas power to green power from the wind and sun.

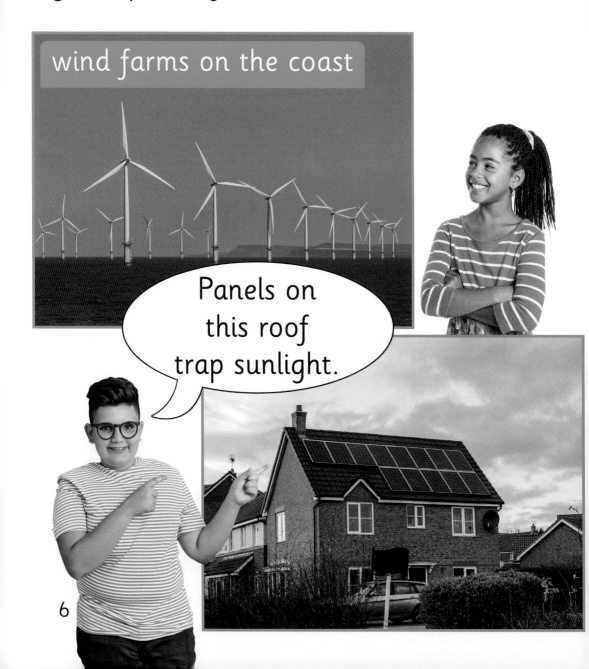

wind farms on the coast

Panels on this roof trap sunlight.

We can put in smarter light bulbs.

We can help lots of trees and flowers to bloom. We can dig ponds to support living things.

tree trunk

trowel

frog

We can travel on trains or by foot. You can scoot down the street.

We can stand up for the planet.

I will send a letter to explain what I think.

I will paint a bright banner.

We can start good habits.

I will fix this, not bin it.

I will compost food scraps.

Three quick things we can do today:
- turn off lights when they are not needed
- have shorter showers
- put litter in the right dustbins.

Be a green star! Stick with it!

Let's help the planet for years to come.

Be a green star

Review: After reading

Use your assessment from hearing the children read to choose any GPCs, words or tricky words that need additional practice.

Read 1: Decoding

- Turn to pages 8 and 9 and look for words with adjacent consonants.
  - Model sounding out **t/r/ee/s**.
  - Point to the following and ask the children to sound them out: **flowers, bloom, trowel; trains, scoot, street**
- On pages 10 and 11 point to the longer words below. Say: Can you blend in your head when you read these words?

  send　　　**paint**　　　**banner**　　　**explain**　　　**compost**

Read 2: Prosody

- On page 10, model reading the first speech bubble, emphasising the pronoun to clarify who is speaking.
- Ask the children to take turns to read the speech bubbles on pages 10 and 11, emphasising the pronouns.
- Read the opening sentences on pages 10 and 11, emphasising **we**. Discuss the effect.

Read 3: Comprehension

- Discuss the meaning of **star** in the context of the book title. Ask: What sort of star is this? (e.g. *a person who stands out for helping the planet*)
- Ask the children what they have done to help the planet, or what they would like to do.
- Ask: Why do you think the author has chosen to write this book? (e.g. *to encourage people to change their habits*)
- Discuss the meanings of words in different contexts.
  - Point to **clear** on page 2. Ask: What does it mean, here? (e.g. *obvious, easy to understand*) Model how it changes meaning in this sentence: It was a clear day. Ask for the new meaning. (e.g. *not cloudy*)
  - Repeat for **stick** on page 12. (means e.g. *don't give up*) What does it mean in: The dog caught the stick? (*a long bit of wood*)
- Look together at pages 14 and 15. Can the children explain how each of the actions shown in the pictures could help the planet?